Getting Around

# By Plane

## Cassie Mayer

Heinemann Library
Chicago, Illinois

Photo research by Tracey Cummins
Designed by Jo Hinton-Malivoire
Printed and bound in China by South China Printing Company
10 09 08 07 06
10 9 8 7 6 5 4 3 2 1

**Library of Congress Cataloging-in-Publication Data**
Mayer, Cassie.
  By plane / Cassie Mayer.— 1st ed.
     p. cm. — (Getting around)
  Includes bibliographical references and index.
  ISBN 1-4034-8390-6 (hc) — ISBN 1-4034-8397-3 (pb)
  1.  Airplanes—Juvenile literature.  I. Title. II. Series.
  TL547.M425 2006
  629.133'34—dc22
                              2005036559

**Acknowledgments**
The author and publisher are grateful to the following for permission to reproduce copyright material:
Alamy p. 21 (Jean Van Straten); Corbis pp. 4 (Macduff Everton), 5 (Stephanie Maze), 6 (Todd Gipstein), 7 (Anthony Bannister/Gallo Images), 9 (Richard Hamilton Smith), 11 (George Hall), 13 (Royalty Free), 14 (George Hall), 15 (Kevin Fleming), 18 (George Hall), 19 (Jeff Vanuga), 20 (George B. Diebold), 22 (Mark Hamilton/zcfa), 23 (Anthony Bannister/Gallo Images), 23 (Royalty Free), 23 (Royalty Free); Getty Images pp. 8 (Banagan), 10 (Gurzinski), 12 (Harvey), 16 (Melford), 17 (Melford), 23 (Harvey).

Cover image of a Stinson Station Wagon aircraft used with permission of Jim Sugar/Corbis. Back cover image of an MD-11 reproduced with permission of George Hall/Corbis.

Every effort has been made to contact copyright holders of any material reproduced in this book.
Any omissions will be rectified in subsequent printings if notice is given to the publisher.

# Contents

Getting Around by Plane ..... 4

What Planes Carry........... 6

How Planes Fly ............. 8

Working on Planes .......... 12

Where Planes Fly .......... 14

Plane Vocabulary........... 22

Picture Glossary ........... 23

Index ................... 24

# Getting Around by Plane

Every day people move from
place to place.

Some people move by plane.

# What Planes Carry

Planes carry people.

cargo

Planes carry cargo.

# How Planes Fly

engine

Planes have engines to help them fly.

wing

Planes have wings to help them fly.

Planes take off on runways.

Planes land on runways.

# Working on Planes

Pilots fly planes all over the world.

Flight attendants help passengers on planes.

# Where Planes Fly

Planes fly over cities.

Planes fly over the country.

Planes fly over mountains.

Planes land on water.

Planes land on ships.

Planes help fight fires.

Planes take you high above
the clouds.

And then they take you back down again.

# Plane Vocabulary

tail

cockpit

wing

engine

# Picture Glossary

**cargo** a large group of items

**flight attendant** a person who helps people during a flight

**passenger** a person who flies on a plane

**pilot** a person who flies a plane

# Index

cargo, 7

flight attendant, 13

passenger, 13

pilot, 12

runway, 10, 11

wing, 9

**Notes to Parents and Teachers**

Airplanes are a form of transportation familiar to children, but how are planes used throughout the world? The photographs in this book expand children's horizons by showing how people move from place to place by plane. Some of the locations featured are Iowa (page 5), Nevada (page 10), Alaska (page 17), Wyoming (page 19), Hong Kong (page 4), Beijing (page 6), South Africa (page 7), the Indian Ocean (page 12), and Switzerland (page 16).

The text has been chosen with the advice of a literacy expert to enable beginning readers success reading independently or with moderate support. An expert in the field of early childhood social studies education was consulted to ensure developmentally appropriate content.

You can support children's nonfiction literacy skills by helping them use the table of contents, headings, picture glossary, and index.